Moods and Emotions

A Handbook About Feelings

by Ruth Shannon Odor
illustrated by John Bolt

Distributed by Standard Publishing
Cincinnati, Ohio 45231.

ELGIN, ILLINOIS 60120

Distributed by Standard Publishing, 8121 Hamilton Avenue,
Cincinnati, Ohio 45231.

Library of Congress Cataloging in Publication Data

Odor, Ruth Shannon.
   Moods and emotions.

   (Living the good life)
   SUMMARY: Examines the positive and negative feelings
everyone has and discusses ways to recognize them in
ourselves and how to respect those of others.
   1. Emotions — Juvenile literature. [1. Emotions]
I. Bolt, John, 1922-   II. Title. III. Series.
BF561.O36   152.4   80-17567
ISBN 0-89565-177-7

Moods and Emotions

A Handbook About Feelings

About *Moods and Emotions*

Moods and Emotions is a handbook about feelings. It is one of a series of books entitled "Living the Good Life."

In this book, written for children from 6 to 12 years old, children's feelings, their *Moods and Emotions,* are explored. These feelings include :
- love
- fear
- joy
- sorrow
- compassion
- jealousy
- wonder
- anger
- loneliness

This book can be used at church or at home. Older children can read it to themselves or to each other. An adult can read the book, a little at a time, to or with younger children. Children will enjoy learning as they think and talk about the ideas and examples given in the book.

Children's feelings are very strong, and sometimes frightening to them, because they have so little experience in handling feelings. This book, *Moods and Emotions,* can help children to explore their feelings, both positive and negative. It can encourage children to rejoice in and treasure their positive emotions; and it can help them to deal with their negative emotions in ways that build strength and develop compassion.

CONTENTS

CHAPTER 1

Many Different Feelings

This is a book about feelings.

God made us with bodies

and with feelings inside our bodies.

Another word for feelings is
EMOTIONS.

There are many different feelings.

Feelings happen to everyone—

MOTHERS,

and FATHERS,

and TEACHERS;

BIG CHILDREN,

and LITTLE CHILDREN,

and MIDDLE-SIZED CHILDREN;

 and even BABIES.

It's okay to have feelings.
Don't be ashamed of them.
Don't try to hide them.

CHAPTER 2

Some Things to Know About Feelings

There are feelings that are pleasant,
  and feelings that are not so pleasant.

Pleasant feelings are called
  positive feelings.

Some positive feelings are
  love,
  joy,
  compassion,
  wonder.

The not-so-pleasant feelings are sometimes
   called negative feelings.

It is not wrong to have these feelings; it is
   normal. Sometimes they are helpful.

Some not-so-pleasant feelings are
   fear,
   anger,
   sorrow,
   jealousy,
   loneliness.

Some feelings come fast.

Some feelings come slowly.

Sometimes feelings last a long time. ➔

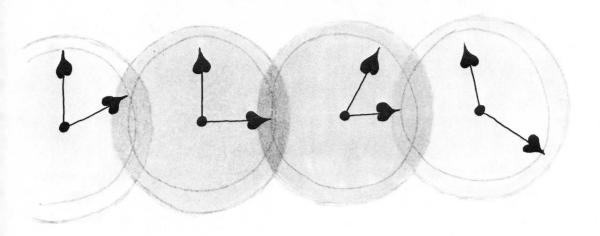

Sometimes they go away quickly. ➔

Some feelings don't just disappear right away. They have nowhere to go. Feelings that have nowhere to go may end up in . . .

a stomach ache,

or a headache,

or a bad dream.

Sometimes feelings come all mixed up. A person may even have opposite feelings at the same time.

(If you want to use an adult word, you call these "ambivalent" feelings.)

I HATE DARLENE AND CHRISTY!

BUT I WISH THEY WOULD BE MY BEST FRIENDS...

Eric is happy about diving off the diving board, but he is scared at the same time.

When you love your brother and hate him at
the same time, don't think. . .

Instead think. . .

Have you ever had opposite feelings at the same time? Get a sheet of paper and a pencil and write down some of those times.

CHAPTER 3

Love

Love is the best of all feelings. Being loved
makes you feel
     safe
     and secure
     and happy.

Our parents' love makes us feel those ways.

Good parents love us just as we are. They love
us all the time—not just when we're good.

We don't have to earn their love. It's just there.

God's love is that way, too. God loves us just as we are. He loves us all the time. He wants us to do right, but he doesn't stop loving us when we don't.

Because you are loved, you can love.

You can love yourself.

You can love others.

And you can love God.

"We love him, because he first loved us."
(1 John 4:19)

Get a sheet of paper and a pencil. First write the names of some of those who love you.

Now write the names of some of those you love.

CHAPTER 4

Fear

Now that you are older, you don't frighten very easily do you? You're not afraid of lots of things that scared you when you were younger. But sometimes you still are afraid. Everyone is.

What are some things you are afraid of now? Get a piece of paper and a pencil and make a list.

Susan is afraid of the dark.

Mike is afraid of Billy, the Bully.

Arlene is afraid the other girls at school will not like her.

Joey is afraid of swimming with his face under water.

Melinda is afraid of storms.

Gordon is afraid of starting fourth grade.

What causes a person to be afraid?

1 Being in a strange place, or having to do something you haven't done before.

Remembering something that happened long ago. **2**

3 Not being sure you are feeling or doing the right thing.

What can you do about your fears?

1. Recognize them, and don't be ashamed of them.

2. Talk about them. Tell Mother or Daddy. Just putting feelings into words helps. And grown-ups understand. They have their fears too.

3 Find out more about what you are afraid of.

4 Sometimes you can keep doing the thing you are afraid of until you aren't afraid any more. Ask someone to help you do it.

5 Make use of fear. It can be very useful—in the right place at the right time.

Afraid to get too near
the edge of the cliff?
Good! You might fall over.

Afraid to get in the deep
water when you can't swim
very well? Good! You
might drown.

6 Talk to God about your fear. God understands. He helps us when we are afraid.

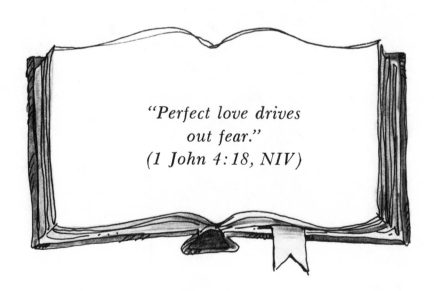

*"Perfect love drives
out fear."*
(1 John 4:18, NIV)

God's love is perfect. So it can drive fear right out "the door."

Don't you suppose Daniel was afraid when he was in that den of lions? What did he do? He prayed to God.

(If you don't already know the story, read it in Daniel 6.)

Don't you suppose David was afraid when a lion attacked his sheep; or when he went out to fight the giant Goliath; or when he fought against the enemy army?

God helped him and took care of him.

(If you don't already know the stories, read them in 1 Samuel 17: 34-50; 2 Samuel 8: 1.)

One of David's prayers was, *"When I am afraid, I will trust in you"* (*Psalm 56: 3, NIV*). Why not learn the words so you can pray them?

God will help you not to be afraid.

CHAPTER 5

Joy

Joy is a good feeling.
Joy is gladness, happiness.

Joy can be bright, quick, and exciting.

Joy can be quiet, slow, and peaceful.

"Rejoice for joy."
(Isaiah 66: 10)

Be glad for moments of joy.
Thank God for them.

CHAPTER 6

Sorrow

Sorrow is a feeling of sadness.

When you are sad, remember. . .

1 Everyone has times of sorrow.

2 Sorrow will not last forever. The sad feeling will get less and less.

(3) Don't blame yourself. Nothing you did made Grandma die or your friend move away.

(4) Jesus understands. He was sad, too. Once He felt so sorry for His friends that He cried.

(If you do not know the story, read it in John 11: 1-45.)

When we are sad, nothing helps as
much as talking it over in prayer.

Do you remember to pray when you are feeling sad?

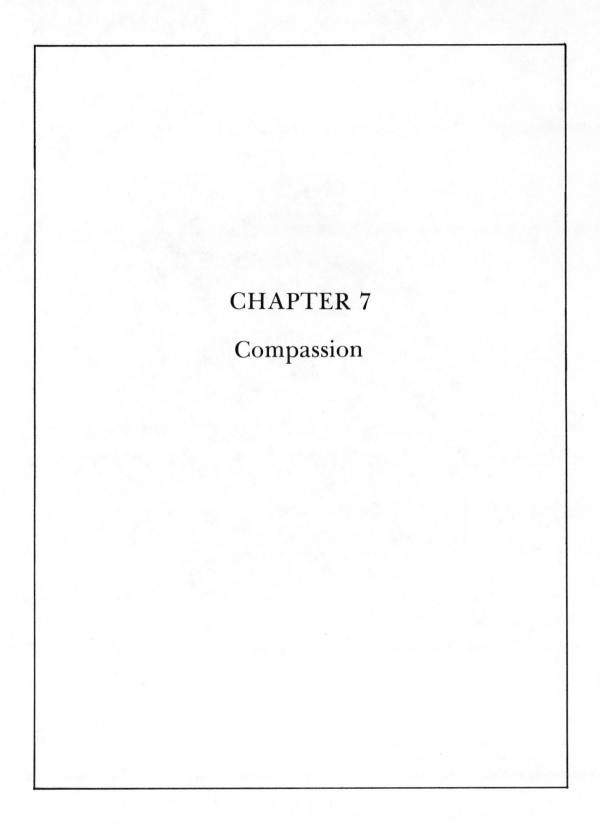

CHAPTER 7

Compassion

Compassion is a feeling of understanding of another person's or an animal's hurt.

When your pet is hurt, you care. You feel as if you hurt, too.

When your friend falls and hurts his knee,
you know how it feels.

    You are sorry for him.

You want to help, and that's part of
compassion. For compassion is more than
understanding how another person feels; it's
wanting to do something about it.

You don't always enjoy the feeling of compassion, but it is an important feeling to have. It means you care.

Jesus felt compassion. He is glad when we do.

"Be ye kind . . . , tenderhearted."
(Ephesians 4:32)

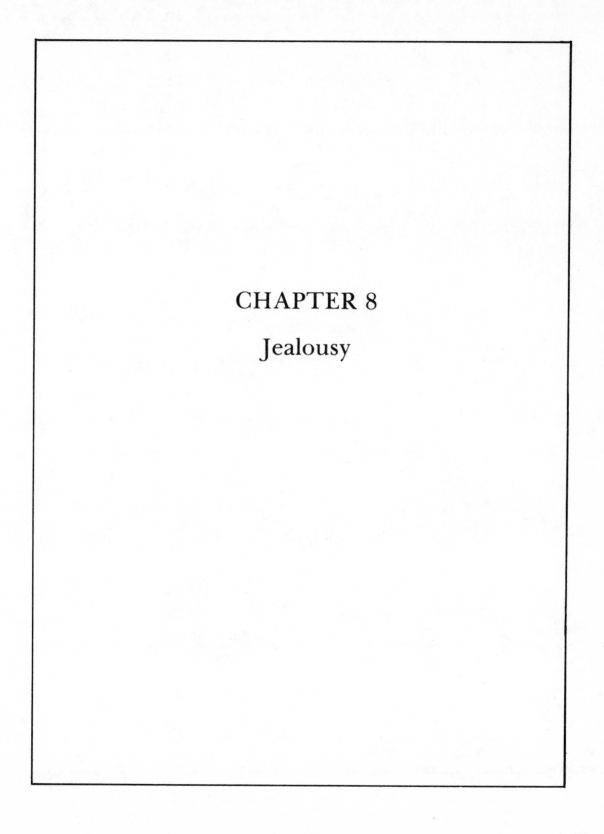

CHAPTER 8

Jealousy

Jealousy is wishing you were being treated as someone else is or wishing you had something someone else has. It's sort of a feeling of half anger and half fear with a touch of resentment stirred in. Everyone feels jealous at times. It just happens.

Sometimes it hurts to have to share Mother's love or Daddy's love.

When you share a candy bar or a piece of gum,

you get less. . .

but when you share love,

you do not get less.

When you feel jealous, here's what to do:

1 Put it into words. Tell Mother or Daddy how you feel and why.

Parents will usually understand. They will be more likely to know what to do when they know how you feel.

(2) Remember that you are a very special person. God made you that way. You have talents no one else has. You can do things no one else can do.

Get a piece of paper and a pencil and write down some times when you were feeling jealous.

What did you do about the feeling?

What could you do the next time to handle your feelings even better?

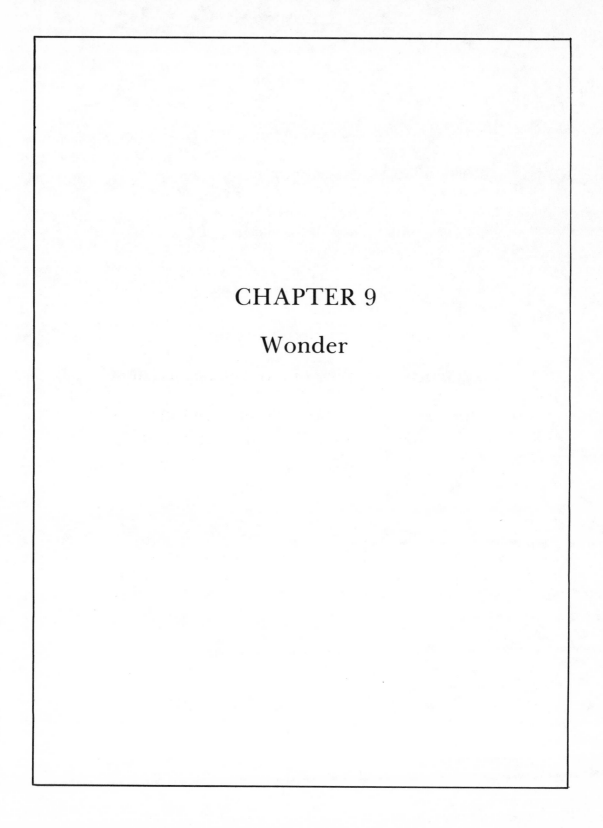

CHAPTER 9

Wonder

Wonder is a very special feeling.

Wonder is a feeling of awe and appreciation.

Sometimes it is part curiosity. You may feel wonder for something special or beautiful. . .

the first violets,

a bird's song,

the way an inch-worm crawls,

green leaves
turning red
in the fall.

Use a pencil and a sheet of paper to write about some things that give you a feeling of wonder.

You may want to draw or paint a picture of one of the things you listed. You may want to write a story or a poem about it.

Be glad for feelings of wonder; enjoy them; thank God for them.

CHAPTER 10

Anger

Sometimes a person feels angry—mad—at someone, at himself, or at the whole world. It is normal to feel angry at times.

Everyone does.

Angry feelings come.

We can't always control their coming. . .

but we can control
what we do
when we are angry.

Don't let the feeling of anger make you do something wrong. Don't let it make you. . .

hurt someone,

or destroy something,

or say something
to hurt someone.

The Bible puts it this way:

"Be ye angry, and sin not."
(Ephesians 4: 26)

How can you handle anger? When you are angry, you can do one or more of these things:

1 Tell someone you are angry and why you are feeling as you do.

2 Work on a solution to whatever has made you so angry.

3 Do something to express your anger in a way that will make you feel better, and make the angry feeling go away.

Draw a picture.

Pound the clay or a punching bag.

Take a walk, or run around a building.

Write about your anger, even if you need to
throw the paper in the fireplace.

Have you ever felt anger? Use a sheet of paper and a pencil to write down some of the times when you felt angry. Also list what you did about your anger.

I was angry when:

Because I was angry, I:

Select one or more of the times you were angry and think about ways you could have handled your anger better.

Use the rest of your sheet of paper to pretend that you are a cartoonist drawing the story of your anger for the Sunday funnies. Draw the cartoons with funny-looking stick figures.

CHAPTER 11

Loneliness

Here am I,
Little Jumping Joan;
When nobody's with me,
I'm all alone.
          —Mother Goose

You know that feeling of loneliness. . . .
Everyone feels it now and then. It seems as if
there is no one but you.

What can you do when you feel lonely?

① Remember that the feeling will soon go away.

② Remember that Jesus is always there. He said, "I am with you always."

3 Find something to do.

4 Find someone to play with or talk to.

CHAPTER 12

Some Things to Do
About Feelings

1 Accept your feelings. (Don't hide them. You have a reason for feeling the way you do.)

2 Recognize your feelings.

3 Understand them.

4 Enjoy the good feelings.

5 Control the way you express a negative feeling.

Think about it. Talk about it. Find a way to handle it.

Listen to your feelings. They help you to understand yourself. They make you do things. They teach you about things you need to know. They help you to understand others and get along with others.

Conclusion

God has made us with wonderful bodies and with all kinds of feelings.

Some feelings make us feel good, and some make us feel bad.

We cannot choose the feelings that come inside of us.

But we can choose how and when to express those feelings.

Learning to recognize our feelings and to respect the feelings of others is a part of growing up the way God wants us to grow.